Paleo Seafood

Most Popular Gluten Free, Delicious and Nutrition-Rich Recipes!

Disclaimer

The ideas, concepts and opinions expressed in this book are intended to be used for educational purposes only. This book is provided with the understanding that authors and publisher are not rendering medical advice of any kind, nor is this book intended to replace medical advice, nor to diagnose, prescribe or treat any disease, condition, illness or injury.

It is imperative that before beginning any diet or exercise program, you receive full medical clearance from a licensed physician. The author and publisher claim no responsibility to any person or entity for any liability, loss, or damage caused or alleged to be caused directly or indirectly as a result of the use, application or interpretation of the material in this book.

Contents

- Disclaimer 2
- Delicious Tuna with Bok Choy 5
- A Tomato-ed Salmon Dish 7
- Rolls Stuffed With Seared Arctic Char 9
- A Tilapian Dish 11
- Tuna Salad with Watercress and Oranges 13
- A Louisianan Catfish Recipe 15
- Salsa with Grilled Shrimp, Pineapple and Melon 18
- Vercruzana with Shrimp 20
- Grilled Scallops with Greek Yogurt Sauce 22
- Cod and Salmon Salad 24
- Sea Vegetables Salad 26
- Baked Fish Casseroles 28
- Scalloped Tacos 30
- Fish Fillets 32
- Pinwheels with Salmon 34
- Fishy Cakes 36
- Sardines Salad 38
- Crispy Casseroles with SeafoodChowder 40
- Seafood Pasta 42
- Sea Food Curry 44
- Salmon and Pickle Tostadas 45
- Chips and Baked Fish 47
- Fishy Burgers 49
- Baked Sea Food with Cod 50
- Shrimp Sandwich 52
- Salmon Garnished With Butter 54
- Fishy Sandwich with Pineapple Slaw 55
- Tuna Spaghetti 57
- Fried Trout 58

Conclusion 60

Delicious Tuna with Bok Choy

Serving Size: 4

Ingredients

Parsley (chopped) – Quarter cup

Dijon mustard (Gluten free) – Quarter cup

Ground pepper – Quarter tsp

Water – 2 tsp

Extra-Virgin olive oil – 1 tsp

Baby bok choy (spruced and sliced vertically) – 2

Tuna, cod, wild salmon or mahi-mahi – Quarter lb.

Preparation Method

1. Set the oven at 450°F.

2. Take a large bowl; and combine parsley, pepper, oil, pepper and mustard in it. When you have mixed it, include bok choy in the bowl too.

3. Take a foil sheet and arrange the bok choy pieces on the foil keep a portion of fish on top of it and pour a table spoon of the sauce. Wrap the foil over the ingredients, close it tightly and keep it on a large baking sheet.

4. Keep the wrapped fish in the oven for about 15 minutes. When you take it out, check whether the fish has turned opaque on the center or not.

5. Place the fish in a serving dish, garnish it with a tablespoon of parsley and serve it to your family.

Nutritional Facts*

Calories – 201

Fat – 7 g

Carbohydrates – 46 mg

Iron – 18% daily value

Vitamin A – 114% daily value

*Nutritional facts are mentioned per serving.

A Tomato-ed Salmon Dish

Serving Size: 4

Ingredients

Sea salt – 1 tsp

Extra-Virgin olive oil – 1 tsp

Ground pepper – Quarter tsp

Garlic cloves (minced) – 2

Fresh basil (sliced) – Quarter cup

Tomatoes (sliced) – 2

Wild salmon fillets – 1 whole or one and a half lb.

Preparation Method

1. Set the grill on heating before starting cooking.
2. Take a small bowl and mix minced garlic and salt in it until it turns into the form of paste. Add oil in it too.
3. Remove pin bones from the salmon and place the fillet on the foil. Smear the garlic mixture on the fillet and sprinkle basil leaves on it too. Put the sliced tomatoes on the fillet too and sprinkle pepper and salt on it too.
4. Put the foil with the salmon on the grill and keep it there for 10 to 12 minutes.
5. After the given time transfer the salmon from the grill to the serving dish. Sprinkle some basil leaves on it and serve.

Nutritional Facts

Calories – 248

Fat – 10 g

Vitamin A – 22% daily value

Vitamin C – 18% daily value

Rolls Stuffed With Seared Arctic Char

Serving Size: 8

Ingredients

Extra-Virgin olive oil – Quarter cup

Sea Salt – 1 tsp

Wild salmon or arctic char (sliced) – 1 lb.

Chard leaves (large) – 4

Cilantro – 32 sprigs

Carrot – 32 slices (1 large-sized)

Tomato slices – 2

Ripe mango (sliced) – 1

Asparagus spears (trimmed) – 16

Sunflower sprouts – 4 ounces

Preparation Method

1. First prepare the fish by slicing it in 3 portions. Marinate it by sprinkling salt on it and refrigerating it for 30 minutes to 1 hour.

2. Take a large sized pan and pour some oil in it and keep it at medium heat. When the oil is heated, put one portion of the fish in it and cook it for about 8 seconds. Turn it over and cook the other side for about the same time. Transfer it to a paper toweled plate and repeat the procedure with the remaining two pieces.

3. Now prepare the hand rolls by separating the chard leaves from the centre rib and placing them in a bowl.

4. Boil the leaves and then shift them in a bowl of ice water so that they can cool off.

5. Spread the leaves on a paper towel so that they can dry off.

6. Now repeat the same procedure with the asparagus.

7. Now take a cutting board and place one piece of chard leaf, 3 fish slice, 4 carrot strips, 2 asparagus spears, 4 tomato slices, 2 mango slices, sprouts, and 4 cilantro springs on it.

8. Wrap the chap leaf around all the ingredients. Close one end of the roll while leave the other end open, like an ice cream cone.

9. Serve it in a vertical position.

Nutritional Facts

Calories – 211

Fat – 14 g

Carbohydrates – 9 g

Vitamin A – 128% daily value

Vitamin C – 47% daily value

A Tilapian Dish

Serving Size: 4

Ingredients

Sea Salt – Quarter tsp

Ground pepper – Quarter tsp

Garlic cloves (minced) – 3

Cherry or grape tomatoes – 1 pint

Extra-virgin olive oil – 2 tsp

Dry white wine – Quarter cup

Tilapia – One and a quarter lb

Olive tapenade – 3 tsp

Preparation Method

1. Take a large saucepan and heat some oil in it. Put the tilapia in it and sprinkle some pepper and salt on it. Cook the fish for about 4 to 6 minutes and make sure it turns golden brown.

2. Take it out on a plate and cover it in a foil so that it can stay warm.

3. Now put t tablespoon oil, wine, tomatoes, and garlic in the pan. Let the ingredients cook for a while and stir them constantly. Keep it on the heat for approximately 5 minutes.

4. Add olive tapenade in the pan too and cook for a little while more.

5. Transfer the fish in the serving pan and serve it with sauce.

Nutritional Facts

Calories – 247

Fat – 11 g

Cholesterol – 71 mg

Vitamin C – 18% daily value

Tuna Salad with Watercress and Oranges

Serving Size: 4

Ingredients

Safflower oil – 1 tsp

Ground coriander – Half tsp

Oranges – 3

Ginger paste – 1 tsp

Sea salt – Half tsp

Apple Cider vinegar – 1 tsp

Black pepper – Quarter tsp

Anise (crushed or chopped) – Half tsp

Watercress leaves or sprigs – 1 cup

Tuna steaks – Quarter lb.

Preparation Method

1. Peel the oranges and separate the pulp from the thin white layer. Squeeze the orange slices and extract all juice from them.

2. Take a bowl and put orange juice, oil, ginger, anise, salt, vinegar and cayenne in it. Stir the mixture gently and keep it on the side.

3. Take a broiler pan and keep it near the oven and set the oven at high heat. Cover the broiler with the foil.

4. Place tuna in the broiler with pepper, salt and quarter spoon aniseed and let it broil for approximately 2 minutes. You can increase the broiling time if you want to soften it more.

5. Add watercress in the orange mixture.

6. Cut the tuna in slices and divide it equally in 4 plates. Top it with the salad and eat it while it is warm.

Nutritional Facts

Calories – 208

Fat – 4 g

Cholesterol – 44 mg

Vitamin C – 94% daily value

A Louisianan Catfish Recipe

Serving Size: 4

Ingredients

Onion (sliced) – 1

Extra-virgin olive oil – 2 tsp + 1 tbsp

Frozen or fresh okra (sliced) – 2 cups

Cajun or Creole seasoning – 2 tsp

Catfish fillets (dry and cut into pieces) – 1 lb.

Preparation Method

1. Set the oven at 450 °F before starting preparations.

2. Take a large bowl and mix onion, okra, oil and Cajun or Creole in it. Pour the mixture on a baking sheet and roast it, all the while stirring it. Keep it there for 20 to 25 minutes. At the end you will see that the vegetables are starting to turn brown and soft.

3. Take a pan and heat some oil in it. When the oil is heated, put the pieces of catfish in it and cook in on medium heat. When the fish starts turning brown, take it out on a serving dish.

Serve the fish with roasted vegetables.

Nutritional Facts

Calories – 288

Fat – 15 g

Cholesterol – 19 mg

Vitamin C – 30% daily value

A Shrimp-Y Ceviche

Serving Size: 8, Half cup each

Ingredients

Lemon juice – 2 lemons

Lime juice – 2 limes

Orange juice – 2 oranges

Cucumber (peeled and diced) – 1 cup

Red onion (chopped) – Half cup

Serrano chilies (chopped) – 2

Sea salt – Quarter tsp

Extra-virgin olive oil – Quarter cup

Cilantro leaves – 1 tsp and extra for garnishing

Tomatoes (diced) – 1 cup

Avocado (chopped) – 1

Raw shrimp (peeled) – 1 lb.

Poaching Liquid

Sea salt – Quarter cup

Water – 2 quarts

Preparation Method

1. Take a large saucepan and put water and kosher salt in it. Boil the liquid mixture. When it reaches its boiling point, include shrimp in it and turn off the stove. Let the shrimp stay in the water for about 3 minutes.

2. After 3 minutes, take shrimps out of the water and spread them on the cutting board. After they cool off, chop them into adequate pieces.

3. Take a bowl and put shrimp in it. Add oranges, lemon and lime juice in it. Plus, put the onion, cucumber and chilies too. Keep the bowl in the refrigerator for an hour.

4. When you take it out of the fridge, add avocado, tomato, oil, salt and cilantro in the bowl too. Keep it at room temperature for about 30 minutes. Garnish it with cilantro leaves and serve!

Nutritional Facts

Calories – 189

Fat – 12 g

Cholesterol – 86 mg

Vitamin C – 48% daily value

Salsa with Grilled Shrimp, Pineapple and Melon

Serving Size: 4

Ingredients

Safflower oil – 2 tbsp

Ripe melon (diced) – 2 cups

Pineapple (diced) – 1 cup

Red onion (diced) – Quarter cup

Sea salt – Half tsp

Ginger (grated) – 2 tsp

Seeded jalapeno (minced) – 2 tsp

Vinegar – 3 tbsp

Red bell pepper (diced) – Quarter cup

Green bell pepper (diced) – Quarter cup

Lime wedges – 4

Fresh mint (chopped) – 2 tbsp

Lettuce leaves – 4

Raw shrimp (peeled) – 1 lb.

Preparation Method

1. Mix t tbsp oil, 1 tsp jalapeno, 1 tsp ginger and shrimp in a large bowl. Cover the bowl and put it in the refrigeration for a day.

2. Take another bowl and mix pineapple, melon, green and red bell pepper, vinegar, mint, onion, and salt in it. Include 1 tsp ginger, 1 tbsp oil, and 1 tsp

jalapeno in too. Keep this bowl in the refrigerator too but only for about 30 minutes.

3. Set the grill on high heat 20 minutes before you plan to eat.

4. Slide the shrimp on the skewers and put in on the grill. Let it stay there until the shrimp turns pink. That will take about 3 minutes per side. Let it cool before sliding it off the skewers.

5. The dinner is ready now it's time to serve. Take a serving tray and spread a large lettuce leaf on it. Place the shrimp on the lettuce and spread salsa on it. Garnish it with lime wedges and mint leaves.

Nutritional Facts

Calories –211

Fat – 8 g

Cholesterol – 168 mg

Vitamin C – 97% daily value

Vercruzana with Shrimp

Serving Size: 4, 1 cup each

Ingredients

Safflower oil – 2 tsp

Onion (sliced) – 1

Garlic cloves (minced) – 4

Tomatoes (diced) – 3

Green olives (sliced) – Quarter cup

Lime (sliced) – 1

Bay leaf – 1

Raw shrimp (peeled) – 1 lb.

Jalapeno peppers (sliced) - 2

Preparation Method

1. Take a non-stick pan and heat some oil in it. put onion, jalapeno leaves, and garlic in it and cook for a while, and stir it constantly.

2. Add shrimp in the pan too and let it cook until the shrimps turn pink. Include tomatoes and olives.

3. Keep the pan on low heat and let the ingredients cook for 2 or 3 minutes.

4. Take it out in the serving dish, remove the bay leaves and garnish with lime wedges.

Nutritional Facts

Calories –192

Fat – 6 g

Cholesterol – 172 mg

Vitamin C – 40% daily value

Grilled Scallops with Greek Yogurt Sauce

Serving Size: 6, 4 scallops each

Ingredients

Ground pepper – Quarter tsp

Safflower oil – 2 tsp

Garlic cloves (grated) – 2

Ginger (grated) – 2 tbsp

Greek Yogurt – 2 tbsp

Apple juice – Quarter cup

Toasted sesame oil – 2 tsp

Red wine – Quarter cup

Lemon juice – 3 tbsp

Cilantro (trimmed) – Half bunch

Dry sea scallops – One and a half lb.

Preparation Method

1. Take out Greek yogurt in a bowl.

2. Take a pan and heat some oil in it and cook garlic cloves and ginger in it until they turn golden-brown.

3. Include Greek yogurt in the pan and cook it for a minute while stirring.

4. Add red wine, sesame oil and apple juice in the pan too and let the pan heat at medium heat. Crush the black beans so that its liquid may secrete. After a while, turn off the heat.

5. Heat the grill before starting the preparations.

6. Put lemon juice, 1 tbsp oil and cilantro in the blender and run it till it turns into a smooth mixture. Take it out in a bowl and toss the scallops in it. Make sure that the mixture covers every inch of the scallop.

7. Split the scallops on 6 skewers and sprinkle some pepper on it. Keep the skewers on the grill and cook it until its edges turn crispy. This will take about 3 minutes per side.

8. Take it out on a serving dish and sprinkle some cilantro springs on it. serve it with the black beans sauce.

Nutritional Facts

Calories –196

Fat – 6 g

Cholesterol – 37 mg

Cod and Salmon Salad

Serving Size: 4

Ingredients

Sea Salt – Half tsp

White-wine vinegar – 2 tbsp

Chipotle Adobo sauce – 1 tbsp

Avocado (diced) – 1

Cherry tomatoes – 2 cups

Water – 2 tbsp

Raw milk cheese – Half cup

Mixed salad green – 10 cups

Wild Alaskan salmon – One and a quarter lb.

Preparation Method

1. Before you start cooking, set the grill at medium heat.
2. Slice salmon into 4 portions and grease it with adobo sauce. Sprinkle some salt on it.
3. Put the salmon on the grill and heat every side for approximately 3 minutes.
4. Take a bowl and put vinegar, chipotle and quarter tsp sea salt in it. Your dressing is almost ready, now put some mixed green salad in it too.
5. Split the dressing and salmon in 4 plates. Garnish it with tomatoes, raw milk cheese and avocado and serve!

Nutritional Facts

Calories – 385

Fat – 22 g

Cholesterol – 91 mg

Vitamin A – 85% daily value

Vitamin C – 60% daily value

Sea Vegetables Salad

Serving Size: 5, 2 cups each

Ingredients

Safflower oil – 2 tbsp

Rice vinegar – 3-quarter cup

Honey (for sweetness) – 2 tbsp

Sea Salt – Half tsp

Carrot (shredded) – 1 cup

Seaweed – 1 cup

Rice noodles – 8 ounces

Red onion (sliced) – 1/3 cup

Cilantro (chopped) – Quarter cup

Red bell pepper (sliced) – 1

Preparation Method

1. Wash seaweed and cook it for a minute or two on stove.

2. Take a bowl and mix sugar, salt and vinegar in it. Include sea weed, bell pepper, cilantro, onion, and rice noodles in the bowl. Your salad is ready!

Nutritional Facts

Calories – 418

Fat – 16 g

Carbohydrates – 58 mg

Vitamin A – 90% daily value

Vitamin C – 64% daily value

Baked Fish Casseroles

Serving Size: 4

Ingredients

Extra-virgin olive oil – 2 tbsp

Dry white wine – 1 cup

Sea salt – Half tsp

Black pepper – Half tsp

Paprika – Half tsp

Onions (sliced) – 2

Fresh thyme (chopped) – 2 tsp

Garlic powder – Half tsp

Raw milk cheese – 1 cup

Grain free sandwich bread – 2 slices

Cod – One and a quarter lb.

Preparation Method

1. Set the oven at 400 °F before starting the cooking.
2. Heat some oil in a pan at medium heat and cook onions in it until they turn golden. Include wine in the pan and cook it for 4 minuted while stirring constantly.
3. Add cod in the pan and sprinkle some salt, pepper and thyme on it. Cover the pan with a foil sheet and place it in the oven. Let it bake for 12 minutes.
4. Now take the remaining ingredients: 1 tsp paprika, oil and garlic powder and mix it with bread. Put the bread mixture and raw milk cheese on top of the fish in the fish and let it bake for 10 more minutes.

5. Take it out of the oven and let it cool. Place it on a dish and serve!

Nutritional Facts

Calories – 328

Fat – 13 g

Carbohydrates – 29 g

Cholesterol – 69 mg

Scalloped Tacos

Serving Size: 4

Ingredients

Extra virgin olive oil – 3 tbsp

Garlic clove (diced) – Quarter cup

Parsley leaves – 3 quarter cup

Red-wine vinegar – 1 tbsp

Oregano leaves – Quarter cup

Bell peppers – 2

Red pepper (crushed) – Quarter tsp

Dry sea scallops – 1 lb.

Paleo Tortillas – 8

Salt – Quarter plus quarter tsp

Preparation Method

1. Put oregano, parsley, garlic, vinegar, 2 tbsp, oil, red pepper, and sea salt in the food processor and run the machine until everything gets crushed properly.

2. Take a pan and heat the remaining oil in it. When it gets hot put bell pepper in it and cook for almost 5 minutes. Take them out in a bowl.

3. Now put scallops and salt in the pan and cook them for about 4 minutes. Include herb sauce in the pan and stir for a while.

4. Now lay down Paleo tortilla in a serving plate and put a quarter cup of scallops and pepper in it. Repeat the same procedure with rest of the tortillas as well.

Nutritional Facts

Calories – 307

Fat – 13 g

Carbohydrates – 30 g

Vitamin A – 59% daily value

Vitamin C – 159% daily value

Fish Fillets

Serving Size: 4

Ingredients

Fish

Fresh ground pepper – Quarter tsp

Sea Salt – Halt tsp

Almond or coconut flour – Quarter cup

Extra virgin olive oil – 1 tbsp

Tilapia, catfish, haddock or any other white fish fillets – 1 lb.

Cilantro pesto

Safflower oil – 2 tbsp

Lime juice – 1 tbsp

Plain Greek yogurt – 2 tbsp

Garlic cloves (minced) – 2

Sea Salt – Quarter tsp

Cilantro leaves – 2 cups

Ground pepper – Quarter tsp

Slivered almonds – 2 tbsp

Preparation Method

1. First prepare pesto. Take a pan and heat some oil in it. When it gets hot, put almonds in it and fry for a little while. After 3 minutes, take the almonds out in a separate plate.

2. Now take out your food processor and put garlic and toasted almonds in it. Pulse it till it turns in a powder form. Include salt, cilantro, lime juice, yogurt, safflower oil, and pepper in it and run it again.

3. Now start preparing fish. Take a bowl and put flour, salt and pepper in it and mix. Immerse the fish fillets in the flour, making sure that every inch of the fillet is properly covered.

4. Heat some olive oil in a pan and start frying the fish fillets in it one by one. Make sure that they are properly cooked and golden in color.

5. Take it out in a serving dish and present it with a table spoon of pesto.

Nutritional Facts

Calories –202

Fat – 12 g

Carbohydrates – 9 g

Pinwheels with Salmon

Serving Size: 4

Ingredients

Lemon juice – 1 tbsp

Extra virgin olive oil – 1 tbsp

Low fat homemade Paleo mayonnaise – 4 tsp

Capers (rinsed and chopped) – 1 tsp

Dijon mustard – 1 tbsp

Thyme (chopped) – 1 tsp

Shallot (chopped) – 1 tbsp

Coconut flour – Half cup

Centre-cut salmon fillet – One and a quarter lb.

Preparation Method

1. Heat the oven at 400 °F beforehand and prepare a baking dish by covering it with cooking spray.

2. Take a bowl and mix mustard, lemon juice, shallot, bread crumbs, thyme and capers in it.

3. Now take a salmon strip and spread a tea spoon of mayonnaise on it then layer it up with 3 table spoons of coconut flour.

4. Roll the salmon fillet such that the rest of the things are covered in the fillet. Put a toothpick through the end so that it can close properly.

5. Repeat the same procedure with the rest of the salmon fillets.

6. Keep all the pinwheels in the oven for about 15 to 20 minutes.

7. Take them out of the oven, remove the toothpicks and serve!

Nutritional Facts

Calories – 342

Fat – 20 g

Carbohydrates – 9 g

Vitamin C – 15% daily value

Fishy Cakes

Serving Size: 4

Ingredients

Onion (chopped) – 1

Extra virgin olive oil – 3 tsp

Parsley (chopped) – 2 tbsp

Dijon mustard – One and a half tsp

Stalk celery (diced) – 1

Egg – 1

Lemon – 1

Coconut flour – 2 cups

Ground pepper – Half tsp

Salmon – 15 ounces

Preparation Method

1. Heat the oven at 450 °F beforehand.

2. Heat some oil in a large pan and put onion and celery in it. Let it cook for some time while stirring it constantly. After some time, add parsley in the pan and remove it from the heat after a minute.

3. Now take the salmon and make it boneless and skinless. Put it in a bowl and include mustard and egg in the bowl. Mix it properly.

4. Include pepper, pan mixture and coconut flour in the bowl too. Combine everything and divide it into 8 patties of equal sizes.

5. Now once again heat some oil in the pan and put the patties in it. Make sure you cook them until they turn golden. Turn them over and cook the other side too. Now transfer the fried patties on a baking pan.

6. Keep the patties in the oven for approximately 15 minutes.

7. Take the salmon cakes out of the oven and serve them with lemon wedges.

Nutritional Facts

Calories –324

Fat – 10 g

Carbohydrates – 21 g

Sardines Salad

Serving Size: 4

Ingredients

Garlic clove (minced) – 1

Ground pepper – Half tsp

Lemon juice – 3 tbsp

Oregano (dried) -2 tsp

Extra virgin olive oil – 2 tbsp

Red onion (sliced) – Quarter cup

Cucumber – 1

Tomatoes – 3

Raw milk cheese – Quarter cup

Kalamata olives (sliced) – 2 tbsp

Sardines (with bones and packed with olive oil) – 2 cans

Preparation Method

1. Chop all the vegetables in and put them in a large bowl. Add pepper and lemon juice and mix them well.
2. Divide them among 4 plates and add a layer of sardines.
3. Serve!

Nutritional Facts

Calories –319

Fat – 19 g

Carbohydrates – 25 g

Vitamin A – 20% daily value

Vitamin C – 35% daily value

Crispy Casseroles with Seafood Chowder

Serving Size: 8

Ingredients

Celery – 1 cup

Almond or coconut – Quarter cup

White potatoes (peeled) – 2

Low fat milk – 1 cup

Safflower oil – 1 tbsp plus 1 tsp

Cod or any other white fish (diced) – 12 ounces

Raw shrimp (peeled and chopped) – 1 lb.

Ground pepper – Half tsp

Leeks (sliced) – 2 cups

Dijon mustard – 1 tbsp

Raw milk cheese (shredded) – 2 cups

Dill (chopped) – 2 tbsp

Coconut flour – Half cup

Crab meat – 8 ounces

Clam juice or seafood stock – 2 cups

Old Bay seasoning – 2 tsp

Preparation Method

1. Heat the oven at 400 °F beforehand.

2. Make use of your Dutch oven by heating a tablespoon of oil in it and cooking celery and leeks in it. Let it stay on the heat for about 3 minutes then add white potatoes, pepper, Old Bay and clam juice in it. Place the lid of the oven and keep it on medium heat until the potatoes turn soft. That will take about 10 minutes.

3. Now add flour, milk and mustard in the mixture and increase the heat while stirring constantly.

4. Include fish, crabs and shrimp too and let it cook for a while. Don't forget to stir.

5. After the fish, crabs and shrimp are tender, remove the mixture from the heat and add raw milk cheese and dill too.

6. Now take a bowl and put breadcrumbs, remaining oil and Old Bay, and cheese in it. Mix the ingredients well.

7. Transfer the cooked mixture in a baking dish and sprinkle the coconut flour mixture over it.

8. Keep the dish in the oven and bake it for half an hour. It will turn golden brown.

Nutritional Facts

Calories –377

Fat – 12 g

Carbohydrates – 31 g

Vitamin A – 17% daily value

Vitamin C – 20% daily value

Seafood Pasta

Serving Size: 4

Ingredients

Garlic cloves (chopped) – 4

White wine – Half cup

Extra virgin olive oil – 2 tbsp

Tomatoes (diced) – 1 can

Cherrystone clams – 1 lb.

Ground pepper – Quarter tsp

Sea Salt – Half tsp

Raw milk cheese (grated) – Quarter cup

Spaghetti squash – 8 ounces

Shallot (chopped) – 1 tbsp

Marjoram (chopped) – 1 tbsp plus for garnishing

Dry sea scallops – 8 ounces

Tilapia or any other white fish – 8 ounces

Preparation Method

1. First prepare the spaghetti squash by cutting it in pieces and baking it for almost 25 minutes.

2. While the spaghettis are baking, heat some oil in a large pan and cook garlic and shallot in it until they turn soft.

3. Include salt, tomatoes and pepper in the pan too. Cover the pan with a lid and let the tomatoes cook for a while.

4. When the tomatoes turn in a semi liquid form, add marjoram, scallops and fish too. Again, cover the lid and let it cook until all the ingredients are properly cooked.

5. Take out spaghetti squash in a bowl and pour the sauce over them. You can garnish it with marjoram and dry milk cheese before serving.

Nutritional Facts

Calories – 453

Fat – 10 g

Carbohydrates – 51 g

Vitamin A – 15% daily value

Vitamin C – 40% daily value

Sea Food Curry

Serving Size: 4

Ingredients

Lemon juice – Quarter cup

Coconut milk – 1 cup

Safflower oil – 2 tbsp

Raw shrimp (peeled) – One and a half lb.

Sea Salt – Half tsp

Madras curry powder – 2 tbsp

Preparation Method

1. Take a normal sized pan and heat some oil in it. Add some curry powder and stir it for a while.
2. Add shrimp in the pan and cook for 3 to 4 minutes. Make sure that the shrimp has turned tender.
3. Include lemon juice, coconut milk and salt too in the pan and turn the heat until it boils. Reduce the heat and let it cook for 2 minutes before you serve.

Nutritional Facts

Calories – 305

Fat – 13 g

Carbohydrates – 14 g

Vitamin A – 25% daily value

Vitamin C – 50% daily value

Salmon and Pickle Tostadas

Serving Size: 4

Ingredients

Avocado – 1

Scallions (chopped) – 2

Mushrooms – 1 can

Cilantro (chopped) – 2 tbsp

Paleo Corn tortillas – 8

Alaskan salmon (skinless and boneless) – 1 can

Pickled jalapenos – 2 tbsp

Cabbage (shredded) – 2 cups

Paleo Salsa sauce (prepared) – 2 tbsp

Plain Greek yogurt – 3 tbsp

Safflower oil – For spraying

Preparation Method

1. Set the oven at 375 °F before staring the preparations.

2. Spray safflower oil on both sides of the tortillas and put them in the oven for 15 minutes. Don't take them out unless they have turned brown.

3. Take a bowl and put salmon, jalapenos, and avocados in it. Take another bowl and mix cabbage, pickles and cilantro in it.

4. Now put mushrooms, salsa, scallions, and plain Greek yogurt in the food processor and pulse in until it turns into fine mixture.

5. Pour that mixture in a bowl and heat it in the microwave until it gets really hot.

6. Now take a piece of tortilla, dip it in the bean mixture and the salmon mixture and pour a spoonful of cabbage salad on the top.

7. Serve!

Nutritional Facts

Calories – 319

Fat – 11 g

Carbohydrates – 43 g

Vitamin C – 60% daily value

Chips and Baked Fish

Serving Size: 4

Ingredients

Safflower oil – 4 tsp

Sea Salt – Quarter tsp

Almond or coconut flour – Quarter cup

Egg whites – 2

Cod – 1 lb.

Russet potatoes – One and a half lbs.

Creole or Cajun seasoning – One and a half tsp

Olive oil - For spraying

Preparation Method

1. Heat the oven at 425 °F.
2. Peel and wash the potatoes, slice them in vertical small pieces and then spread them on the baking sheet and keep them in the oven for about 30 to 35 minutes. Take them out when they turn golden.
3. Take another dish and put flour, salt and Cajun seasoning in it.
4. Take another bowl and whisk the egg whites in it.
5. Now take a piece of fish and dip it in the flour first and then coat it in egg white.
6. Spray cooking oil on both sides of the fish and keep it in the oven.
7. When the fish turns brown and crispy, take it out of the oven and serve with baked chips.

Nutritional Facts

Calories – 325

Fat – 5 g

Carbohydrates – 45 g

Vitamin C – 58% daily value

Fishy Burgers

Serving Size: 4

Ingredients

Sea salt – Quarter tsp

Ground pepper – Quarter tsp

Cilantro (chopped) – 2 tbsp

Extra virgin olive oil – 1 tbsp

Red onion (chopped) – 2 tbsp

Ginger chopped) – Half tsp

Salmon fillets – 1 lb.

Preparation Method

1. Chop the salmon in quarter inch pieces. Be careful; don't turn them into mushy fillets.
2. Put them in a large bowl and toss in onions, cilantro, salt, ginger, and pepper. Mix them without damaging the fillets.
3. Divide the fish into 4 patties and keep them in the refrigerator for about 20 minutes.
4. Take a large pan and heat some oil in it. Fry the patties in the oil and then buns too. You can heat buns in the microwave also. To enhance its taste, you can add some sauce in the burgers too.

Nutritional Facts

Calories – 239

Fat – 13 g

Carbohydrates – 2 g

Baked Sea Food with Cod

Serving Size: 4

Ingredients

Grape tomatoes – 1 pint

Dry white wine – Half cup

Extra virgin olive oil – 1 tsp

Shallot (chopped) – 1

Sea Salt – Half tsp

Thyme (chopped) – 1 tsp

Cod – One and a quarter lbs.

Spanish chorizo (diced) – 2 ounces

Ground pepper – A pinch

Preparation Method

1. Heat the oven at 425 °F.

2. Take a saucepan and heat some oil in it. Put shallot, thyme and chorizo in it and cook for a while. Stir constantly.

3. Include tomatoes, salt and quarter cup wine in the saucepan too. Keep it on medium heat and let it cook for a while. Don't forget to stir.

4. Now put the fish in the baking pan, spray salt and pepper over it and top it with tomato mixture and quarter cup wine. Keep the dish in the oven for about 15 to 20 minutes.

5. Check after a while if the fish is cooked properly then serve.

Nutritional Facts

Calories – 293

Fat – 8 g

Carbohydrates – 18 g

Vitamin A – 15% daily value

Vitamin C – 20% daily value

Shrimp Sandwich

Serving Size: 4

Ingredients

Plain Greek yogurt – 2 tbsp

Red onion (sliced) – Quarter cup

Chili powder – 1 tsp

Paprika – Half tsp

Tomatoes – 4

Red cabbage (shredded) – 2 cups

Safflower oil – 4 tsp

Ground pepper – Quarter tsp

Aioli – 2 tbsp

Raw shrimp (peeled) – 1 lb.

Paleo burger buns – 4

Dill pickle relish – 2 tbsp

Preparation Method

1. Heat the grill before you start cooking.
2. Take a bowl and mix aioli, pickle, cabbage and yogurt in it.
3. Add chili powder, 2 tea spoons oil, pepper, paprika, and shrimp in the bowl.
4. Put remaining oil in another bowl and with the help of a cooking brush, spread it inside the buns.
5. Spread the shrimps on the grill and keep them there until they turn pink.

6. Toast the buns on the grill too until they turn a bit crispy.

7. Now assemble the sandwich by laying a layer of onions, tomatoes and cabbages on the bun. Top it up with a generous quantity of grilled shrimp and the other bun.

Your sandwiches are ready!

Nutritional Facts

Calories – 322

Fat – 10 g

Carbohydrates – 32 g

Vitamin A – 25% daily value

Vitamin C – 45% daily value

Salmon Garnished With Butter

Serving Size: 4

Ingredients

Almond butter – 1 tbsp

Lime juice – 2 tbsp

Sea salt – Half tsp

Ground pepper – Quarter tsp

Chili powder – Quarter tsp

Lime zest (grated) – Half tsp

Unsalted papayas – 2 tbsp

Salmon fillets – 1 lb.

Preparation Method

1. Marinate the papayas by placing them in a bowl with lime zest, chili powder, lime juice and butter.
2. Heat some oil in a pan and put salmon fillets in it, sprinkle some salt and pepper on the fillets. Cook the fillets until they turn brown from both sides.
3. Transfer the salmon from the pan to a plate and pour the papaya mixture into the pan. Keep it on the stove until the butter melts.
4. Pour some sauce oven the salmon fillets and serve!

Nutritional Facts

Calories – 259

Fat – 17 g

Carbohydrates – 2 g

Fishy Sandwich with Pineapple Slaw

Serving Size: 4

Ingredients

Coconut flour – Quarter cup

Safflower oil – 4 tsp

Salt – Quarter tsp

Plain Greek yogurt – 2 tbsp

Rice vinegar – 2 tsp

Homemade Paleo mayonnaise – 2 tbsp

Red pepper (crushed) – Quarter tsp

Cod or haddock – One and a quarter lbs.

Cajun seasoning – Half tsp

Pineapple chunks – 1 can

Grain free sandwich bread – 8 slices

Preparation Method

1. Take a bowl and mix vinegar, yogurt, red pepper, mayonnaise, and pineapple in it.

2. Take out coconut flour in a dish. Chop fish into normal sized pieces, sprinkle some Cajun seasoning over it and dip it on the flour.

3. Take a saucepan and heat some oil in it on medium heat. Put the fish in the saucepan and cook it until both sides of the fish turns golden.

4. Transfer fish to a plate. Take two pieces of toasted bread, spread some pineapple slaw over it and sandwich fish between the two bread pieces.

5. Serve while sandwiches are hot!

Nutritional Facts

Calories – 372

Fat – 9 g

Carbohydrates – 42 g

Vitamin C – 44% daily value

Tuna Spaghetti

Serving Size: 4

Ingredients

Garlic (minced) – 2

Extra virgin olive oil – 2 tbsp

Tomatoes (diced) – 1 can

Anchovies – Half cup

Spaghetti squash – 8 ounces

Basil leaves – 2 tbsp

Red pepper – Quarter tsp

Tuna – 1 can

Preparation Method

1. Boil the spaghetti squash or prepare it by following the instructions mentioned on the packet.

2. Heat some oil in a pan and cook garlic, anchovies, red pepper, and tomatoes in it. When tomatoes start leaving their water, add tuna in the pan too and cook for a while until the fish gets tender.

3. Divide spaghetti in four plates, pour some sauce on every plate and sprinkle some basil leaves. Your spaghettis are ready! Serve while they are still warm.

Nutritional Facts

Calories – 349

Fat – 8 g

Carbohydrates – 50 g

Fried Trout

Serving Size: 4

Ingredients

Coconut flour – 3 quarter cup

Sea salt – Half tsp

Buttermilk – Half cup

Pine nuts – 2 tbsp

Shallot (minced) – 1

Trout fillets – 4

Unsalted almond butter – 2 tsp

New Mexican chili powder – 2 tbsp

Organic chicken broth – 1 cup

Safflower oil – 4 tsp

Gluten free Worcestershire sauce – One and a quarter tsp

Preparation Method

1. Take a bowl and mix buttermilk, salt and a tea spoon of chili powder in it.
2. Put coconut flour in another shallow dish.
3. Take a piece of trout fish, dip it in the coconut flour and then in the other mixture. Make sure every side of the fish is covered with both mixtures.
4. Now heat some oil in a sauce pan and fry the fish in it until it turns golden brown. Repeat the process with all fish fillets.

5. When you take out the fish, put shallot, chili powder and almond butter in the sauce pan and cook for a while, stirring it constantly.

6. Include Worcestershire sauce and chicken broth in t he sauce pan and cook for a few more minutes.

7. Pour this sauce over the fish and garnish it with pine nuts.

Nutritional Facts

Calories – 378

Fat – 19 g

Carbohydrates – 19 g

Vitamin A – 29% daily value

Conclusion

You don't need to stick to tasteless diets when you can maintain your health with various Paleo recipes mentioned in this eBook. These recopies are healthy and delicious, something that is extremely hard to accomplish with any other diet regime. So, enjoy tasty healthy food!

Made in the USA
Lexington, KY
25 April 2014